December 2012

To my beloved

friend.

BJL

jodi hills

TRISTAN PUBLISHING
Minneapolis

To Cindy,
who let me go home from my fourth grade
sleepover, and didn't tell anyone that I was
homesick. She made me laugh and helped
me cry, and showed me that being a friend,
may just be that simple.

Hills, Jodi
Friend / written by Jodi Hills.
     p. cm.
ISBN 978-0-931674-84-6 (alk. paper)
1. Friendship. I. Title.   BF575.F66H55 2010
177'.62--dc22   2010011272

TRISTAN PUBLISHING, INC.
2355 Louisiana Avenue North
Golden Valley, MN 55427

ISBN 978-0-931674-84-6
Printed in China
Second Printing

I really like
who I am
with you...

I hope that doesn't sound bad to say...

I mean it more as a compliment to you,

more of a "thank you" really.

You free me to be this person who laughs and

cries and feels and enjoys and loves.

What a relief
to be myself,
without performing,
or worrying...

just being and becoming who I am...

That's some gift...
I hope I'm returning it...
because you know what,

I really like
who you are
with me.

You - in a world filled
with so many people,
living so many lives -

it's you.

It's amazing that
your one life
can mean so much
to mine.

It's wonderful how
much your life matters.

It matters to me if
you're excited or scared,
or looking for something.

Out of all the billions

of faces, I see you.

I feel your strength,
and it helps me
feel my own.

I hear a laugh in a crowd,
and I smile, because I know
it came from you,
and it makes me feel special
to recognize the joy that
comes from your one life.

Out of all the countless drummers,
I hear you. What a beautiful noise.

And yet, we can say nothing, and
know exactly what the other means.

We've seen each other through
beginnings and ends.

You are a constant in this impermanent place.

Thank you for all of it…
the sounds
and the peace
and the fun
and the calm
and the strength.

Thank you for making car rides shorter.

Thank you for being the person I go to
when I need to start the conversation,
"Ok, but don't tell anybody..."
and I know that you won't.
And thank you for entrusting me with the same

Thank you for your
ever willing hands,
that are just there to help me,
and not trying to fix me.

Thank you for nodding,
when even I know
I'm not making any sense.

And thanks for telling me
about that thing dragging
from my shoe.

Thanks for abiding by the unwritten rule that only one of us can freak out at a time... and for allowing me the extra turns.

Thank you for the inside jokes
and for laughing at my repeats.

Thank you for knowing things -
with no exhausting explanations needed.
Thanks for being around on Tuesdays,
and not just special occasions.

You're really good
at all the little things,
and that's a pretty big deal!

Thank you for giving me a part of you,

and bringing to life a part of me.

I think that's what a true friend does,

not only gives you a part of themselves,

but gives you more of yourself -

lets you be yourself.

I know you're thinking,
"anyone could have done it,"
and you're right, everyone can,
just not everyone does...

But you did, you do...

and for this, my friend,

I make you a promise,

when the daring others look at me,

really look at me, on one of my best days,

they will see you...and they will know,

I am only better for having such a friend.

It makes a difference,
you know,
the goodness created
between friends.
It grows and it travels,
between and beyond.

Some might say, "All of this goes without saying, doesn't it?"

Maybe it does, but I don't want to take that chance.

Every day, you need to know

how special you are to this world,

and thankfully, to me!

Not to be all dramatic…

We'll talk tomorrow about nothing

and everything. But before we get

deep into conversation about how

cool it is to be like us,

I wanted to tell you that

it's great to be your friend.